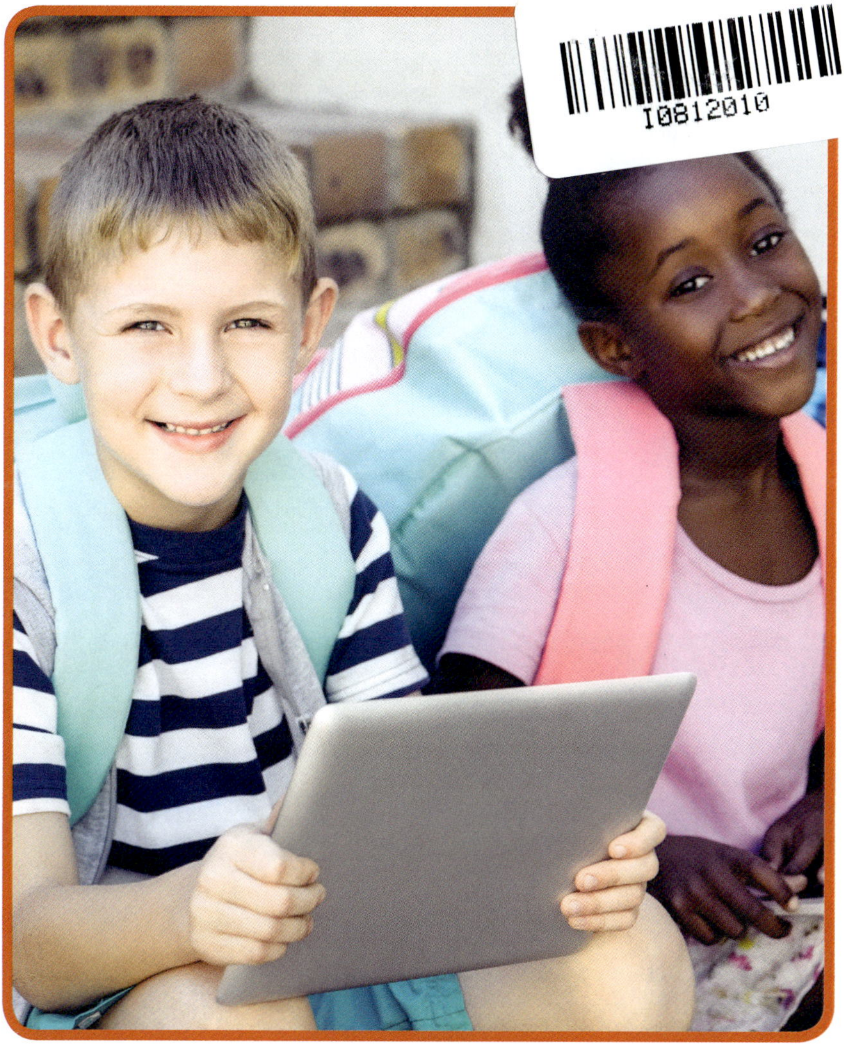

It is good to share.

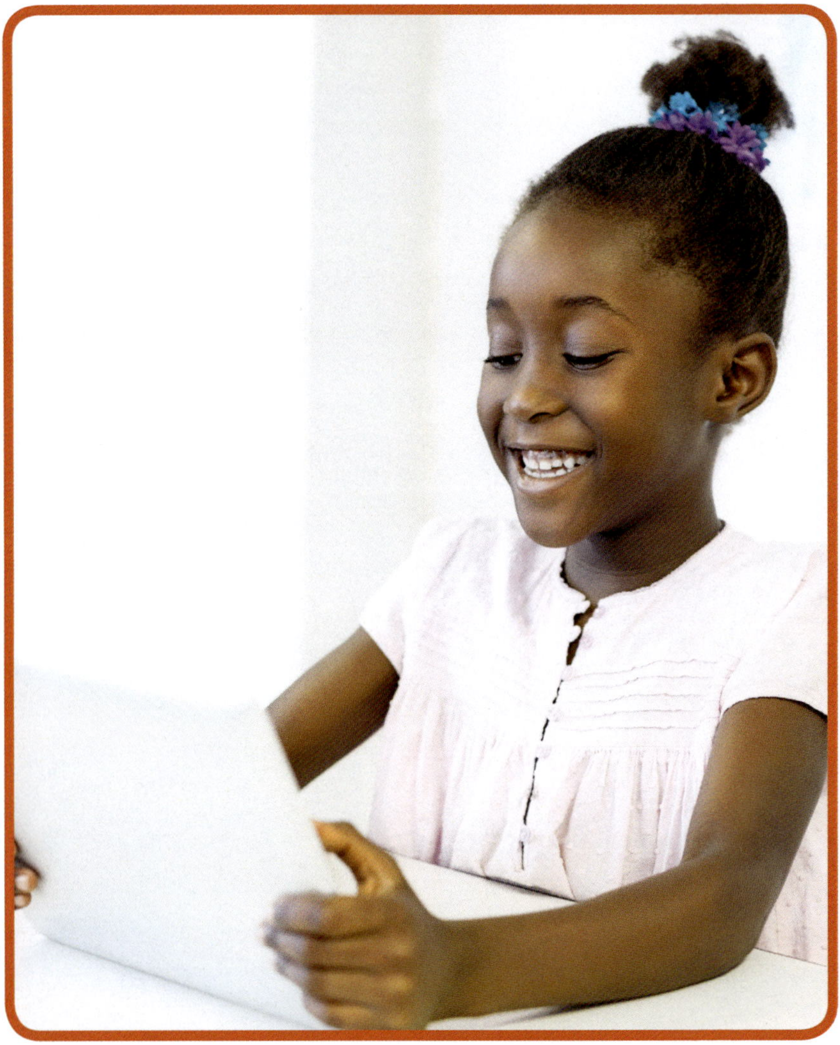

I use the tablet.

We Can Share

CIVIC VIRTUES

Rory McCallum

CIVICS FOR THE REAL WORLD™

Rosen Classroom™

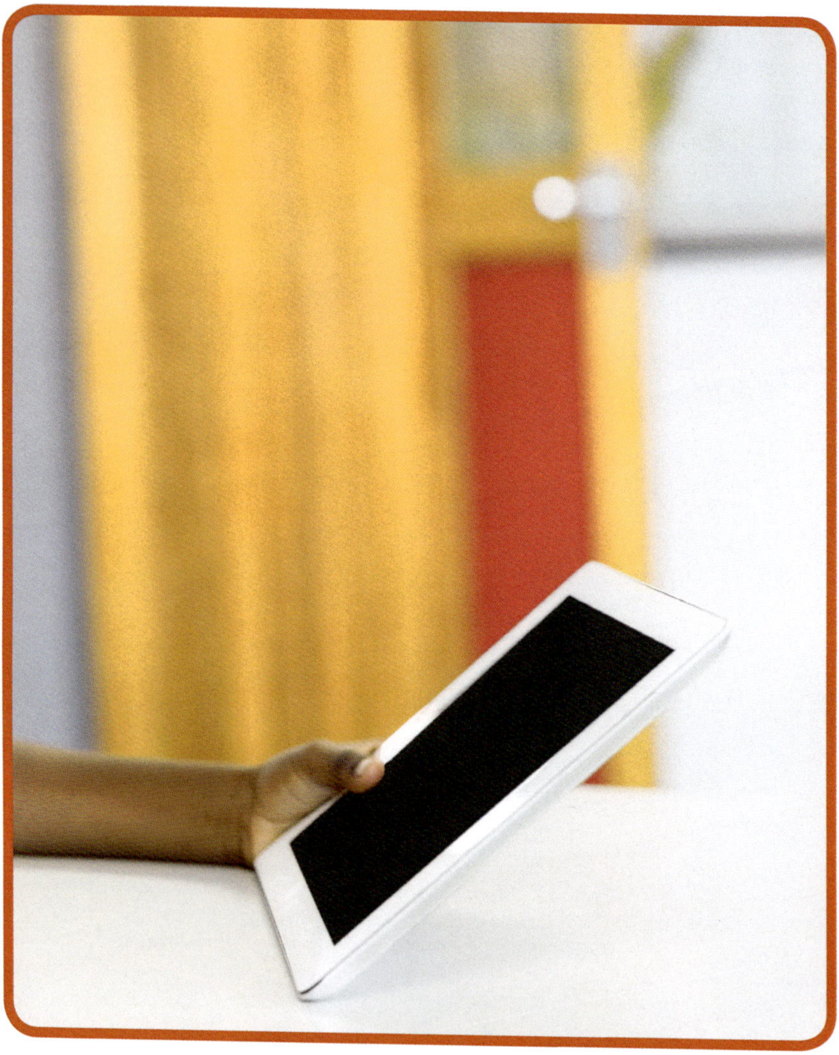

My class has a tablet.

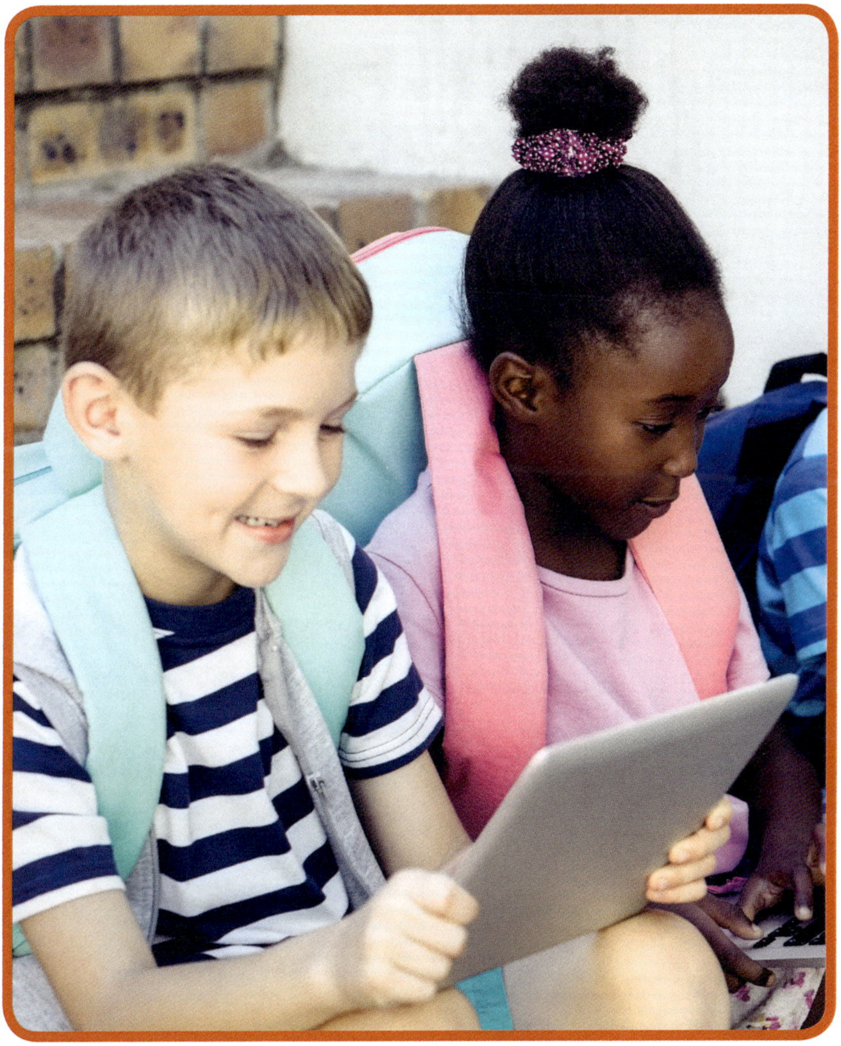

We all want to use it!

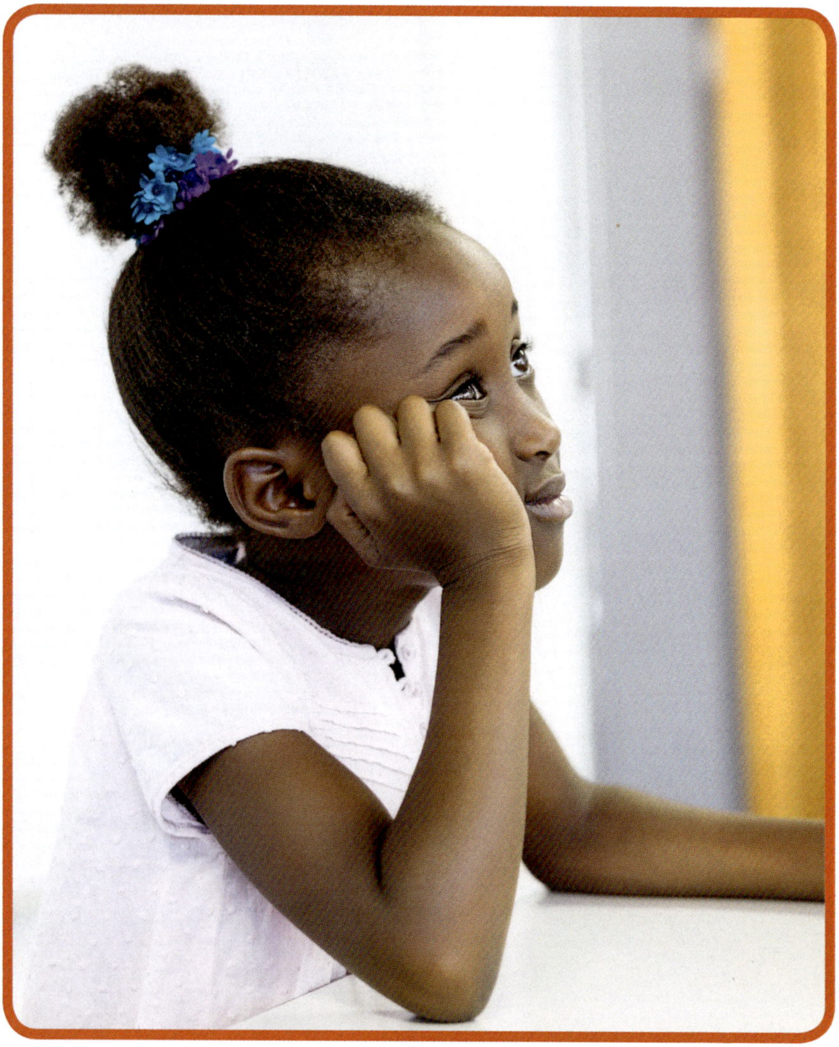

We fight over the tablet.

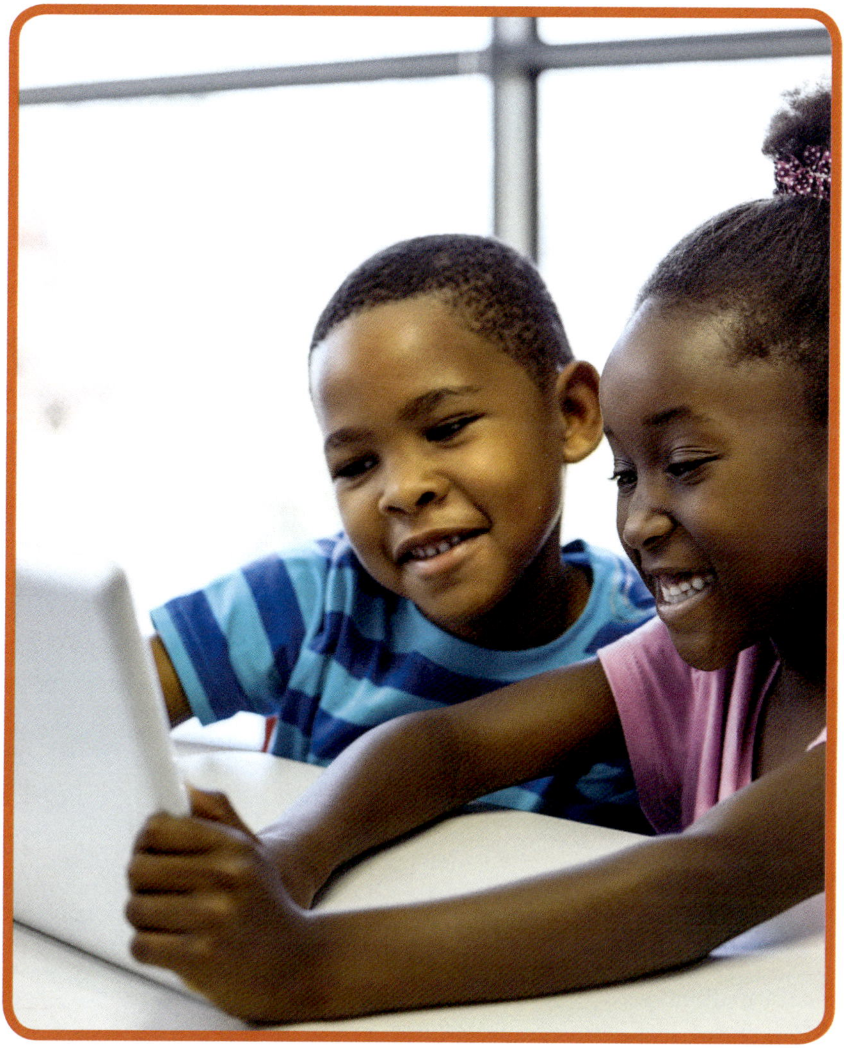

I share with Tim.

WORDS TO KNOW

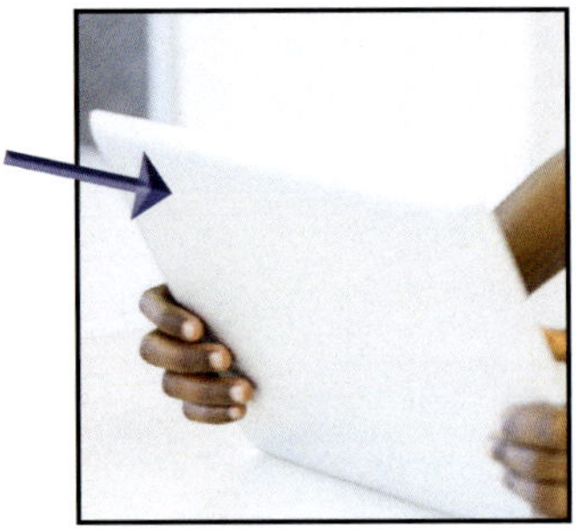

tablet